The
Royal Palace
of Seville

The Royal Palace of Seville

Juan Carlos Hernández Núñez
Alfredo J. Morales

Scala Publishers
in association with
Aldeasa S.A.

The Royal Palace of Seville
Text © Copyright Alfredo J. Morales 1999
Photography © Fotografías Arenas, 1999
© Santiago Moreno, 1999, pages 9, 19, 42, 44, 68, 73

First published in 1999
by Scala Publishers Ltd
Northburgh House
10 Northburgh Street
London ECIV OAT

ISBN-10: 1-85759-201-8
ISBN-13: 978-1-85759-201-6

Edited and designed by Grapevine Publishing Services
Translated from the Spanish by Nicholas Chadwyck
Printed and bound in Spain
10 9 8 7 6 5 4 3

Photographic credits: All the photographs used in this book were supplied by
Fotografías Arenas, except for those on the pages above, that are credited to
Santiago Moreno.

Contents

THE REAL ALCÁZAR

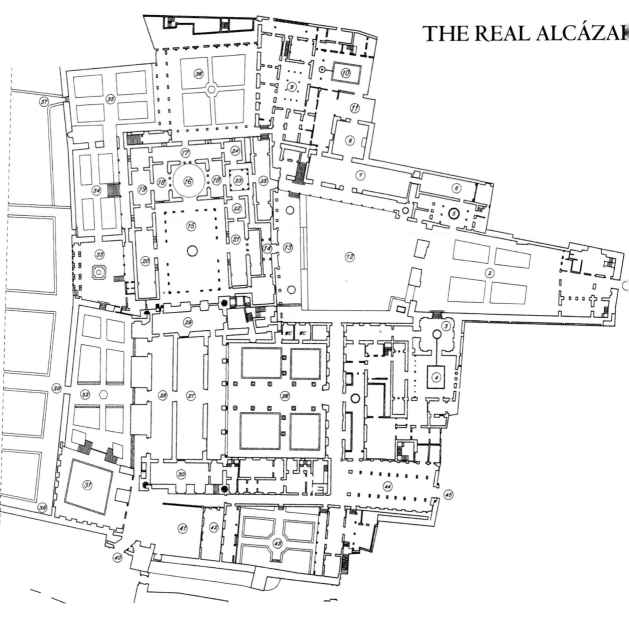

GARDENS

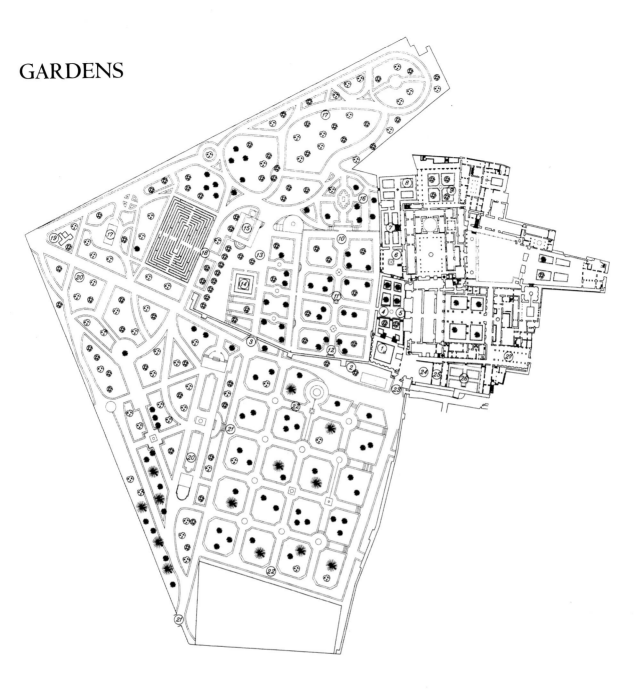

The Moorish Stronghold

The Real Alcázar (Royal Palace) in Seville is probably the most ancient of the European royal residences still serving their original purpose. It consists of a complex and dazzling assemblage of buildings dating from different periods and having different architectural styles, the result of a process of demolition, refurbishment and reconstruction that has continued uninterrupted almost until the present day.

The origins of the Real Alcázar go back to the ninth century, when in the reign of Emir Abdul Rahman II a military stronghold was raised on the site of a Visigothic basilica. Later, in the time of Caliph Abdul Rahman III, it was consolidated as a governor's residence (Dar al-Imara), thus serving the dual function of palace and fortress. It took the form of an irregular rectangle set on a north-south axis. Although the building included the present-day Patio de Banderas (Courtyard of Flags), it was not large; nonetheless, according to the Muslim chronicler Al-Himyari, its high stone curtain wall and solid defensive towers ensured its impregnability. Along the northern side, the wall was set with turrets; this can be seen today in the Plaza del Triunfo and Calle Joaquín Romero Murube. The other three walls were either rebuilt, as on the eastern side, or were altered and concealed by other buildings that now form part of the Real Alcázar. The principal entrance to the palace was a main gate, now filled in, and today situated between two later towers in Calle Joaquín Romero Murube. (From here it can be seen that the surrounding wall, with its irregular header and stretcher stonework, started at a lower level.) This original main gate consists of a horseshoe arch beneath a brick lintel, framed by a rectangular *alfiz* (decorative frieze). It was formerly overhung by a

Left: The Alcázar walls from the Plaza del Triunfo

Opposite: Aerial view

Opposite: Gateway to the former
Dar-al-Imara palace

Right: Main gateway to the
Patio de Banderas

cornice, of which only remnants of moulding can be seen today. The capitals on the
inner face of the arch date from Almohad times.

On the northern side of the enclosure is the gateway to the Patio de Banderas, a
space that must originally have functioned as a parade ground in front of the
governor's residence. This entrance is a much-altered stone arch surmounted by a
tilework plaque with the royal coat-of-arms and the words Reales Alcázares (Royal
Palaces). This was designed at the end of the last century by the Sevillian scholar
and historian José Gestoso. The machicolation and crenellations, made of bricks,
date from a later period than the wall itself.

This early nucleus of the Real Alcázar was one of the first architectural projects
carried out by the emirs of Córdoba. After the fall of the Córdoban caliphate, when
Muslim Spain was divided among Reyes de Taifas (petty kings), Seville came under
the rule of the Abbadid dynasty (1023-91). The prosperous kingdom of Seville was
determined to emulate the power and sumptuousness of Madinat al-Zahra, near
Córdoba, capital of the Umayyad caliphs; the Real Alcázar in Seville became the
focus of gatherings of the most celebrated poets of the time and the new courtly
residence became a centre of the arts in Spain. The new buildings required to house
the ever more complex and ceremonious life of the court were extended westwards
towards the banks of the Guadalquivir. The palace complex came to be known as al-
Qasr al-Mubarak (Blessed Palace). It was now entered on the western side through a
fortified gateway set with towers and known today as the Arquillo de la Plata (Silver
Keyhole). The residential and private apartments were grouped around a large

courtyard laid to gardens with surrounding walkways and a pool. These apartments, which underwent alteration in the Almohad period, stood on the site, which, by the fifteenth century, would be occupied by the Casa de la Contratación de las Indias (House of Trade with the Indies).

Main gateway to the Patio de Banderas

Nearby, and built in a very different style, stood the public and ceremonial part of the palace. It consisted of a series of rooms arranged around a large domed hall; these, like gleaming stars, mirrored the constellation of the Pleiades. Architecturally and in terms of ornamentation, the hall, known as the Turayya (Pleiades), emulated the palace complex of Madinat al-Zahra: sumptuously carved capitals and fine marbles were incorporated into the building in an attempt to evoke the prestige of that Ummayad capital. Ornamentation featured figurative and plant motifs together with lengthy inscriptions of verses praising the palace by poets of the court of Abbad al-Mutamid, second king of the Abbadid dynasty. Most notable among these were poems composed for the Turayya by the Sicilian poet Ibn Hamdis, which express the belief that the hall was without equal, even among the Persian palaces or yet even those of Solomon, with its brilliant rays of sparkling sunlight that acted like a palette serving the hand of the artist. It was in these magical surroundings, in which architecture and poetry became indivisible, that Abbad al-Mutamid, the poet-king, lived the best years of his life; he always felt a special predilection for his 'blessed palace', yearning for it whenever he was away, especially in the sad days of his exile in Agmat, that inhospitable North African land to which he was banished by the Almoravids. From his prison, he cried:

If I could only spend one more night
between pool and garden,
in the olive-groves, a legacy of grandeur,
where turtle doves sing and little birds warble;
in the Zahir, sheltering in a gentle rain,
while the Pleiades wink at us and we wink at them,
and the Zahi with its Sud al-Suud hall, watching us with envy,
because envy is love's constant companion;
it may be easy, it may be difficult;
everything depends upon the will of God.

In the fourteenth century, this magnificent palace would provide shelter for Muhammad V, the overthrown Nasrid sultan of Granada, and his court poets. When Muhammad regained power and retook possession of his residence in the Alhambra in Granada, Abbad al-Mutamid's palace in Seville became the model for the new Cuarto de los Leones (Suite of the Lions) in the Alhambra. Shortly after, a similar process took place, albeit in reverse, when Don Pedro, or Peter the Cruel decided to renovate the Turayya to make it the centre of official life in his palace, converting it into what is now known as the Salón de Embajadores (Ambassadors' Hall). Craftsmen were sent by Muhammad V of Granada to grace the walls of the old Abbadid palace with ornamental plasterwork and tile decoration in the new Nasrid style.

Puerta and Patio del León

Work on the conversion of the Turayya into the Palacio del Rey Don Pedro (Palace of Peter the Cruel) began in 1364. The main entrance was once known as the **Puerta de la Montería** (Gate of the Hunt). Its present name, the **Puerta del León** (Gate of the Lion), dates from the 19th century and is derived from the heraldic lion, in a tilework panel, that is set above the gate beneath a defensive chute or machicolation. This panel, made in 1894 after a design by José Gestoso, shows the lion with a crown, a cross and a flag, and a broad sash bearing the inscription *'Ad Utrumque'* (Prepared For All). The panel is surrounded by a knotted cord. It replaces an older painting on the same theme.

It is not known what link may have existed between this painting and the low-relief heraldic motifs on the curve of the arch, of which there are traces on the left-hand impost. These reliefs probably disappeared in the course of the alterations that were made to the gateway over the centuries. The gateway itself now consists of an arch framed by a rectangular alfiz that meets the top of the keystone but then cuts across the curvature of the arch on each side. Originally the arch must have been of the horseshoe type.

The Puerta del León leads into the **Patio del León** (Courtyard of the Lion), which was laid to gardens between 1936 and 1937 by the architect Juan Talavera. Facing the entrance is part of the Almohad defensive wall. (The façade is of masonry but the rear of the wall displays unfaced rubble.) It is pierced by three arches. The two outer arches were originally of the horseshoe type but were converted into round arches by cutting through the imposts; these were left open as a result of Juan Talavera's alterations in the 1930s.

Puerta del Léon

Of special interest are the decorative intersecting arches around the left-hand arch. These decorations formed part of the refurbishment carried out in Almohad times to the patio of the al-Qasr al-Mubarak. The central arch lies directly opposite the façade of the Palacio del Rey don Pedro. Traces of the original heraldic decorative carvings – medallions surrounded by interlaced lines embracing the coats-of-arms of Castile and León and of the Order of the Sash, which was founded by Alfonso XI – can be seen on the jambs and voussoirs of the arch.

Within the Patio del León once stood a theatre, the Corral de la Montería (Enclosure of the Hunt), in which were performed some of the most outstanding plays of the Spanish Golden Age. The theatre was begun in 1625 to a design by the Milanese architect Vermondo Resta but was completely destroyed in a great fire on 3 May 1691.

The left side is bounded by the rough-hewn stone wall of the old Moorish governor's residence. It is pierced by a small arch that provides access to the **Sala de la Justicia** (Chamber of Justice). This is built on a square plan, following the pattern of the Muslim *qubba* (mausoleum). The walls are partly covered with stucco decoration and the ceiling is wood-framed.

Opposite: Patio del León
(above), and a detail of the walls
in the Patio del León (below)

Right: Gateway between the
Patio del León and the Patio de
la Montería

Opinion on the origins of the room is divided: some believe that it was built on ancient Almohad foundations and date its present shape to the first half of the fourteenth century, during the reign of Alfonso XI; others maintain that because of its ornamentation and the Arabic inscriptions on the walls, which are similar to those found in the Palacio del Rey Don Pedro, it must have been built by Don Pedro in the second half of the fourteenth century. The inscriptions read: '*Allah is the refuge, Bliss, Continual prosperity, Praise be to Allah for his goodness.*' The laudatory legend inscribed on the upper frieze makes reference both to Don Pedro, for whom the palace was constructed, and to its majestic quality: '*Let praises be sung to the noble lord of this incomparable house.*' According to some authorities, Don Pedro dispensed justice in this room from a throne placed against one of the walls, which would explain its name. Tradition also has it that the Sala de la Justicia was the scene of the murder of Don Pedro's stepbrother Fadrique, Maestre de la Orden de Santiago (Master of the Order of Santiago), who was accused of committing adultery with his queen. However, it is more likely that the murder took place in one of the former rooms of the ancient Palacio de Yeso (Stucco Palace), which adjoins the Sala de la Justicia.

Each wall of the Sala de la Justicia has a tripartite arrangement, with a central arch flanked by niches. The arches are framed by stucco panels with plant motifs (of a type known as *ataurique*) and inscriptions. The ornamentation on the east wall is particularly fine; the underside of the arch is covered with exuberant *ataurique*, while the lintel above supports blind multifoil arches. The door jambs are

Above and opposite:
Sala de la Justicia

decorated with sixteenth-century ceramic tiles. Two stucco friezes run round the walls. The lower frieze incorporates small blind arches and coats-of-arms, and the upper frieze has real and false windows, the real ones covered by latticework screens. Dados, which do so much to enrich other rooms in the palace, are lacking in the Sala de la Justicia, although the lower part of the walls was originally painted and some traces of colour can still be seen. The wood-frame ceiling is notable for its double mitred hip rafters and is particularly noteworthy for the carving on the pendentives at each corner and the central octagon with its pine-cone boss decorated with *muqarnas* (decorative stalactites). The room has a marble floor. In the centre is a small fountain from which water runs away along an open channel into the **Patio del Yeso**.

The Patio del Yeso (Stucco Courtyard) originally formed part of the Palacio de Yeso built in the Almohad period. The courtyard is almost square and has a large pool in the middle. A three-tier gallery runs along its southern side. In the central tier, sturdy brick pillars support a large scalloped arch, the spandrels of which are covered by a decorative mesh of rhomboid forms of a type known as *sebqa*. The sections on either side of the main arch comprise a triple arcade, supported on columns with Moorish capitals; the arcades' multifoil arches support areas of openwork *sebqa* decoration. This decorative scheme, also seen in the gallery on one of the longer sides of the patio, is considered to be a forerunner of designs that would later become widely used in both Nasrid and Mudéjar architecture. Inside the portico is the entrance to a large rectangular chamber with alcoves at each end,

Patio del Yeso, north side (above) and south side (opposite)

where some traces of Mudéjar painting remain. This entrance consists of two horseshoe arches supported on a central column, each surmounted by a window filled with a latticework screen. The entrance is of a more advanced design than that of the door on the north side of the courtyard, where the three-tier gallery, with its alternating voussoirs and upper horseshoe-shaped openings, recalls an earlier style that was common in the palace of Madinat al-Zahra and became widespread during the Abbadid period.

Patio de la Montería

The **Patio de la Montería** (Courtyard of the Hunt) fronts the Palacio del Rey Don Pedro. It is the shape of an irregular rectangle and is built on two levels separated by flowerbeds; the lower level, nearest the palace, has a number of fountains. During the seventeenth century it was proposed to line the other three sides of the courtyard with an arcade so as to give a harmonious appearance to the whole. Antón Sánchez Hurtado, master builder of the Real Alcázar, undertook this project, but the arcade was built only on the western side by 1588. It consists of two tiers of columns, Tuscan on the lower level and Ionic on the upper, and supports masonry arches. In the eighteenth century, this scheme was followed on the eastern side of the courtyard, where a row of blind arches adorns a building used for various purposes, to which light is admitted by a series of windows and balconies.

On the eastern side of the courtyard is a suite of three rooms known as the **Cuarto del Almirante** (Admiral's Suite). The stone beside the main entrance was placed there by members of the Academy of Science to commemorate a visit to the Real Alcázar by Charles IV and his wife Maria Louisa in 1796. Their visit was

West gallery of the Patio de la Montería

Virgilio Mattoni, *The Last Hours of Saint Ferdinand* (1887)

celebrated by sumptuous festivities: various temporary but lavish structures were erected and repairs were carried out to the doors, windows, stained glass and decorations of the palace to render it fit to receive the king.

The three rooms forming the Admiral's Suite probably developed from a group of chambers added to the al-Qasr al-Mubarak, Abbad al-Mutamid's palace, in the eleventh century and were refurbished during the sixteenth and seventeenth centuries. Of the al-Qasr al-Mubarak, one courtyard remains; this was converted by the Almohads into a garden, which can be seen in the adjacent offices of the Andalusian Department of Public Works. It was here that Christopher Columbus was received by Isabella of Castile after his second voyage to the Americas, and where on 14 January 1503 she founded the House of Trade with the Indies, whose function was to regulate the traffic of goods and people to and from the New World, administer the fleets and teach the art of seamanship. If it was thanks to trade with the Indies that Seville became the main port in Europe, it was education that, in the words of the Italian humanist Pietro Martire d'Anghiera, made it the 'House of the Ocean'. It was unquestionably one of the most important seafaring and scientific research centres in sixteenth-century Europe.

Related to all this activity was the production of one of the first seafaring maps, drawn by the cartographer and explorer Juan de la Cosa in the late 15th century, and the creation in 1512 of the Padrón Real, a prototype of marine cartography, which underwent continual development, extension and correction as the result of news that was brought in by navigators, who made notes in the detailed logs that they kept of their journeys.

All this new knowledge was increased by expeditions of a more or less scientific nature, resulting in such epoch-making events as the discovery of the Pacific on an expedition led by Vasco Núñez de Balboa, or the first circumnavigation of the globe, which started out under the command of Ferdinand Magellan and was completed after his death when the *Victoria* arrived in the port of Sanlúcar in 1522, under the command of Juan Sebastián Elcano.

Among the important figures who worked at the Casa de la Contratación de las Indias were such eminent navigators as Amerigo Vespucci, Alonso de Chaves and Andrés García de Céspedes, as well as the cosmographers Alonso de Santa Cruz, Diego Ribero, Rodrigo Zamorano and Jerónimo de Chaves, and the nautical writers Francisco Falero and Pedro de Medina.

Today but three rooms of the Casa de la Contratación de las Indias remain. The **Sala del Almirante** (Admiral's Hall), seat of the court of the Castilian admiralty, is a large rectangular room with beams supported on corbels. It houses an important collection of nineteenth- and early twentieth-century paintings. Most noticeable, owing to its colossal size, is *Las Postrimerías de San Fernando* (*The Last Hours of St Ferdinand*), painted by the Sevillian artist Virgilio Mattoni in 1887. The painting depicts the death of the king in the Alcázar of Seville in 1252 as described in the *Estoria de España*, a contemporary chronicle written by his son Alfonso X (The Wise). Next to this is a portrait of Francisco de Asís, consort of Isabella II, painted by Bernardo López Piquer in 1864. At the head of the room hangs *La Toma de Loja* (*The Taking of Loja*) by Eusebio Valldeperas, first exhibited in 1862; the painting depicts Boabdil, king of Granada, surrendering the keys of the city to the Ferdinand V in 1486, watched by the Gran Capitán, Gonzalo Fernándes de Córdoba. There are also portraits, painted by Carlos Blanco in the early decades of the nineteenth century, of Ferdinand VII and his fourth wife Maria Christina of Naples, parents of Isabel II, and the infanta Maria Louisa. The portraits of the French king Louis-Philippe of Orléans and his wife Marie Amélie, their son Antoine, Duke of Montpensier, and his wife the infanta Marie Louise of Bourbon are by Franz Xaver Winterhalter. These important examples of nineteenth-century court portraiture came from the palace of Miramar in San Sebastián. At the end of the room is a painting by Alfonso Grosso that depicts the inauguration of the Spanish-American exhibition in Seville on 9 May 1929. The royal family – Alfonso XII and Victoria Eugenia of Battenburg, their son the infante Alfonso and daughters the infantas Christina and Beatrice, and their uncle Charles of Bourbon – appear with other figures, among them General Berenguer and General Primo de Rivera, the Marquis of Nervión and José Calvo Sotelo, who played vital roles in Spanish political life in the early twentieth century.

The Sala del Almirante leads into a room known either as the **Capilla** (Chapel) or **Sala Capitular** (Chapterhouse). Its religious connotations derive from the Madonna of the Seafarers, the altarpiece that dominates the room, but it also functioned as a meeting place for officials attached to the Casa de la Contratación de las Indias, for whom the stone bench running around the walls was intended. Built to a square plan, the room has a magnificent sixteenth-century coffered ceiling, with octagonal and star-shaped caissons, which display strong Mudéjar influence. In 1967 the room underwent far-reaching restoration in the course of which the bench was rebuilt and the wall hangings were renewed. These are embroidered with the coats-of-arms of the Admirals of Castile, from the original admiral Ramón Bonifaz in 1248 to Admiral Enríquez, a member of the royal house of Castile, in 1492. In place of honour, at the centre of the room facing the altarpiece, is the coat-of-arms of Admiral Christopher Columbus.

As part of the programme of restoration carried out in the 1960s, a reproduction of the framework of the Virgen de los Mareantes (Madonna of Seafarers) altarpiece, which had disappeared in the 19th century, was put in place. The painting

itself, by the German-born artist Alejo Fernández, dates from 1535 and is the earliest work in which a religious theme is related to the discovery of the New World. It has an unusual iconography. The Madonna shelters a group of Native Americans under her cloak; in the right foreground is a group of figures who may depict the Holy Roman Emperor Charles V, Ferdinand and Isabella (the Catholic Kings) and members of the Casa de la Contratación de las Indias; on the left, under the Madonna's right hand, are Christopher Columbus and Martín and Vicente Pinzón, who accompanied Columbus on his first voyage to the New World. Below them are the various types of vessel that made up the Spanish fleet in the early 16th century. On the left of the central panel is a depiction of St James the Apostle, patron saint of Spain, at the battle of Clavijo, and St Sebastian, protector of the army. On the right side are St Elmo, a patron saint of sailors, and St John the Evangelist, the special object of Isabella's devotions, depicted writing the Book of Revelations on the island of Patmos.

The Sala del Almirante also leads into **Room III**. This now houses an important collection of fans made between the seventeenth and twentieth centuries. Apart from those of traditional European type, the collection includes some Oriental examples; among the most interesting are Japanese fans of asymmetrical shape decorated with scenes of daily life. Particularly noteworthy among the European examples are the lace fans of French manufacture and fans signed by painters or miniaturists such as Basire, Ravault, Rebours, Boudet and Dupont-Watteau.

The large townscape in Room III depicts the great procession of the Entombment, which would wind through the streets of Seville at regular intervals

Great Procession of Holy
Entombment, details

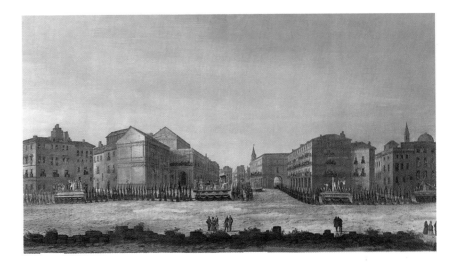

Main stairway, detail of tile dado (opposite) and ceiling (right)

on the Saturday evening in Holy Week. The procession would be made up of various brotherhoods of penitents with their respective floats, who would have been taking part in processions throughout the week. The painting is of considerable historical interest as it shows, albeit with some licence, a view of Seville as it appeared in the mid-19th century. The procession is depicted against the backdrop of Seville Cathedral, with the main doors still unfinished (they were not completed until 1927) and the building on the south-western corner that later became the cathedral museum and was also completed in the early decades of the twentieth century. Also visible is the Calle de los Alemanes and the Plaza de San Francisco, which at the time still had its portico is now dominated by the city hall, with its ancient passage leading to the convent of San Francisco; here also is the arcade designed by Hernán Ruiz the Younger in the mid-sixteenth century and demolished in the nineteenth century. The procession comes to an end at the Plaza del Duque, where the church of San Miguel and the palace of the Duke of Medina Sidonia (neither of which still stand) can be seen.

To the right of the door to the Sala del Almirante is the **main staircase** of the Royal Palace. Three flights supported by a double arch resting on a pair of Ionic columns lead to the upper floor. The staircase walls are faced with a dado of mid-17th-century Sevillian tiles which were originally in the convent of the Madre de Díos. The stairwell has a late sixteenth-century octagonal carved wooden ceiling resting on pendentives, the caissons decorated with floral motifs. On the wall is a large painting of the Immaculate Conception; although it has been attributed to Juan de Roelas, it is in fact the work an anonymous Sevillian painter dating from the early seventeenth century.

Upper Floor

The oldest rooms on the upper floor date from the second half of the fourteenth century and formed part of the Palacio del Rey Don Pedro. Other rooms were added in the fifteenth century, during the reign of Ferdinand and Isabella; in the sixteenth century almost all the rooms were altered to serve the ceremonial and other functions of the court more effectively. The only rooms on the upper floor that retain their original form are the Dormitorio del Rey Don Pedro and the Sala de Audiencias. All the others underwent major alterations, although most still have their original wooden ceilings. The rooms are richly furnished, mainly with nineteenth-century pieces, to render them fit for use by members of the royal family when they stayed at the palace or performed official duties in Seville.

Because they are used as royal apartments, these rooms are not open to the public. Nevertheless, some of them will be described here. The rooms comprising the **Cuarto de la Reina** (Queen's Suite) are remarkable for their wooden ceilings. The room that now serves as the entrance hall is topped with a wooden ceiling of

Left: Royal bedroom, ceiling

Opposite: Family dining-room, ceiling

the hip rafter type made in the fifteenth century, as demonstrated by the coats-of-arms and the motto *Tanto Monta* that adorn it.

Also dating from the fifteenth century is the octagonal wood-frame ceiling, supported on pendentives in the room leading into the **Oratorio de los Reyes Católicos** (Oratory of the Catholic Kings). The oratory, with its ribbed vault ceiling, is dominated by a magnificent tilework altarpiece made by Francisco Niculoso Pisano in 1504, an innovative Italian craftsman who worked in Seville in the late fifteenth and early sixteenth centuries. The central portion of the altarpiece consists of a scene of the Visitation framed by the Tree of Jesse showing the genealogy of Christ. The altar front bears a scene of the Annunciation and the whole is crowned with a head of Christ. On the left are the coat-of-arms of the Spanish monarchy and the symbols of Ferdinand and Isabella , the yoke and sheaf of arrows accompanied by the motto *Tanto Monta*, and a wide variety of grotesques and symbolic motifs. The whole altarpiece is a richly colourful masterpiece of Renaissance ceramic art; the different elements are depicted in blue and white chiaroscuro on a yellow background, except in the landscape in the Visitation scene and the surrounding border, which have a dark blue background.

Above: Francisco Niculoso Pisano, altarpiece (1504), Oratorio de los Reyes Católicos

Opposite: Dormitorio del Rey Don Pedro

The **Dormitorio del Rey Don Pedro** (Bedchamber of Peter the Cruel) is one of the few parts of the upper floor of the Real Alcazár that dates back to the fourteenth century. It is square in plan and originally contained two sleeping alcoves. The mosaic of interlaced motifs that covers the dados is original, as is a large part of the profuse stucco decoration on the walls above them, although some of this stucco was added in the mid-sixteenth century. The wood-frame ceiling, which has an interlaced motif at the centre, is an extraordinary example of Mudéjar woodcarving of the first half of the fifteenth century.

The bedchamber leads into the **Mirador de los Reyes Católicos** (Viewing Gallery of the Catholic Kings), a large rectangular room whose outer walls are pierced with horseshoe arches supported on columns, from which gardens and the upper gallery on the south side of the Patio de las Doncellas (Courtyard of the Maidens) can be seen.

These arches have masonry parapets with painted Mudéjar designs and Gothic upper windows with the emblems of the Reyes Católicos (Catholic Kings). The ceiling is another outstanding example of Mudéjar artistry. The room was

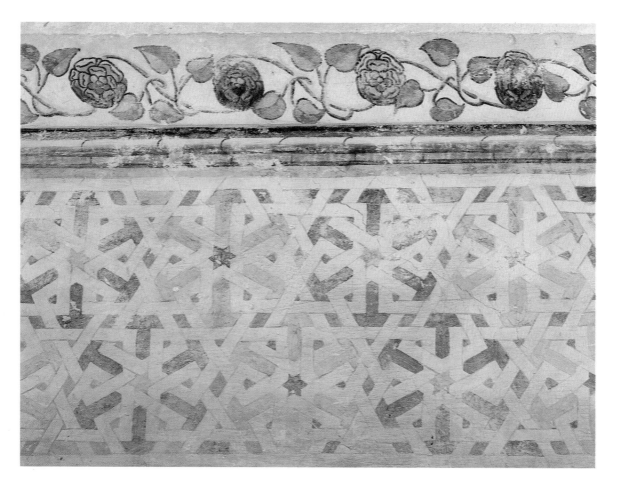

Above: Mirador de los Reyes Católicos (detail of painting)

Opposite: Sala de Audiencias

fundamentally altered during the 16th century but it has now been restored to its original appearance.

The most sumptuous room on the upper floor of the Real Alcazár is the **Sala de Audiencias** (Audience Chamber), which also forms part of the fourteenth-century Mudéjar palace. The walls have a tripartite arrangement with arches supported on marble columns of different colours with Moorish and Renaissance capitals. The north side of the room adjoins the front of the palace, from which it is separated by a narrow gallery beneath a vaulted ceiling decorated with *muqarnas*. The dados are covered with splendid and original *alicatado* mosaics with polychrome designs, while the rest of the walls are enriched with intricate stucco featuring plant and calligraphic motifs and *muqarnas*. The ceiling, of wood with lattice decoration, was rebuilt by José Gómez Otero in 1909.

Later Courtyards

To the west of the Patio de Montería is an area once known as the Corral de las Piedras (Enclosure of Stones); it was here that the new kitchens and offices of the Real Alcazár were added in the seventeenth century. This area was reorganized in the eighteenth century, when it was converted into the residence of the Asistente de Sevilla (Assistant of Seville). Here Pablo de Olavide would hold his literary gatherings (some of the most celebrated in late eighteenth-century Spain), very much in the French style in those enlightened times. Completely restored in 1967, the area is organized around three courtyards.

The **Patio del Asistente** (Courtyard of the Assistant) is reached by a passage adjacent to the stairs to the upper floor of the palace. With its twin galleries, it is one of the few examples of the traditional Castilian patio to survive in Seville. The lower gallery has marble Tuscan columns; these support the upper gallery, which is identical to the lower one except that it has chamfered timber supports instead of columns. The courtyard houses a small collection of tiles dating from the fifteenth to the twentieth centuries, which exemplify a variety of decorative techniques, some of local origin, others imported from Delft, in Holland, and adapted and reinterpreted by Sevillian ceramicists. Of particular importance is a tile attributed to Francisco Niculoso Pisano, all that remains of an altarpiece depicting the Coronation of the Virgin that Pisano made for the palace in 1504. Many of the exhibits were produced in the workshops in the Triana district of Seville in the late nineteenth and early twentieth centuries. During this period, Sevillian pottery underwent a renaissance; old techniques were revived and new ones introduced, and Art Nouveau ornamentation was combined with traditional styles. An example of traditional tile design is a panel depicting the Adoration of the Magi, executed by Manuel Corbato in the late nineteenth century, and which can be seen in one of the display cases.

Since 1969 the next courtyard has been known as the **Patio de los Levíes** (Courtyard of the Levites); this name refers to the courtyard's Mannerist

Above: Patio de los Levíes

Opposite: Patio del Asistente

portico, which came from the former Casa de los Levíes (House of the Levites) in the Jewish quarter of Seville. The portico consists of four arches supported on columns and pilasters. The arches are raised on tall, narrow pedestals and rest on square mouldings; this adds to the delicacy of the whole. Further adornment is provided by other mouldings in layers around the arches and on the entablature (architrave, frieze and cornice) above them, oculi (round holes) in the spandrels of the arches and by the use of white and veined marble. In the middle of the courtyard stands a pedestal fountain with four lion-head spouts from which a channel carries water to a basin of mixed rectilinear and curvilinear design. This is also fed by another channel from a fountain at the end of the courtyard facing the portico. On one side of the courtyard is a tilework panel showing the Virgin Mary surrounded by cherubs' heads: a fine work from Seville workshops specializing in Baroque pottery.

From the Patio de los Levíes, a door leads to the **Patio de los Poetas** (Courtyard of the Poets), also known as Patio de Romero Murube, which was named after the writer who was the curator of the Royal Palace from 1934 to 1969. The intimate charm and coloration of this patio evokes the romantic tradition of Sevillian domestic architecture.

Palacio del Rey Don Pedro

The **Palacio del Rey Don Pedro**, named after the king of Castile and León for whom it was built, is one of the most important secular buildings in the Mudéjar style, in which Christian and Islamic elements are fused. The palace is important not only because it was the first major architectural project to be undertaken by the Castilian monarchy; it also represents the combination of a number of different tendencies in Moorish art that were current in the Iberian peninsula at the time.

For his palace Don Pedro called on the skills not only of artists and craftsmen from Seville and Toledo but also of others who were sent from the Nasrid kingdom of Granada by Sultan Muhammad V, whom Don Pedro had aided in regaining possession of his throne. These artists and craftsmen invested the building with a wide variety of decorative styles that embody artistic development in Spain between the thirteenth and fourteenth centuries. The palace clearly reflects the fascination that refined Islamic culture held for the Christian Spanish monarchy; it also stands as a monument to the co-existence of the two religions, as demonstrated by the Kufic inscriptions on its walls, which extol the greatness of 'Sultan Don Pedro', the sovereign protected by Allah.

Palace façade, overlooking the Patio de la Montería

Main façade, upper floor gallery

Built between 1364 and 1366, the Palacio del Rey Don Pedro incorporates part of the former al-Qasr al-Mubarak, the 'Blessed Palace' that Abbad al-Mutamid had built in the eleventh century. According to the canons of Islamic architectural practice, the Palacio del Rey Don Pedro was divided into two areas, one for private use and the other for official use, each being clearly differentiated according to their function. While the private area had as its focal point the Patio de las Muñecas, the official area was organized around the Patio de las Doncellas.

In this larger, official area the decoration is more sumptuous, particularly in the throne room, or Sala del Almirante, a symbol of magnificence and royal power. Abbad al-Mutamid's palace had been built mainly on one floor; the Sala del Almirante, with its magnificent façade and two upper rooms supported on tall arches, was added above it. These two upper rooms, of a type generally used for storage, would later become the nucleus of the upstairs apartments built in the reign of the Reyes Católicos for use as living quarters during the winter months. With the arrival of the house of Habsburg, the whole palace underwent further alteration and refurbishment to meet the needs of the court and to bring its older parts and accoutrements into line with the new aesthetic currents of the sixteenth and seventeenth centuries. During the eighteenth century, the most significant alterations came about as the result of work carried out to repair damage caused by the Lisbon Earthquake of 1 November 1755 and a disastrous fire that began on the afternoon of 1 December 1762. The alterations made in the nineteenth century

Above: Main façade, windows

Opposite: Salón de Embajadores

followed no clear pattern and are sometimes contradictory; work was carried out to convert the Real Alcázar into a residence for the Dukes of Montpensier. The palace was also reorganized and the use of space rationalized, with new galleries and other areas being added to the existing private quarters. In addition, a programme of work was undertaken to restore the palace to its former splendour. This work, beset by disagreements over the general approach to the restoration of the building, was to continue throughout the twentieth century.

The main entrance to the Palacio del Rey Don Pedro is on the southern side of the Patio de la Montería. The monumental façade is divided into three sections. Those on either side are the result of a series of alterations and refurbishments. As we can see today, they are of brickwork and comprise an upper and a lower portion. The lower level consists of a gallery with four arches within decorative frames, supported on chamfered pillars. These galleries were discovered in the mid-twentieth century during the course of restoration, when the wall in which the arches were embedded was knocked down. Above this gallery is a high parapet supporting a second arcade. This was built after the Moors were expelled from Granada in 1492, as shown by the pomegranates decorating the rectangular frame of the central window of the right-hand wing. The gallery has a tripartite structure, with a central arch flanked by three arches on marble columns within a tall *alfiz*, with *sebqa* decoration between the tops of the arches and the border of the *alfiz*. Above them runs a wooden frieze with the emblems of Castile and the following words:

La dicha, la paz, la gloria, la generosidad y la felicidad perpetua (para su dueño) ('Happiness, peace, glory, generosity and perpetual felicity (to the master of the house)'). Above this on each side are the roofs of the upper floor apartments. In the centre is the graceful cube of the Sala de Audencias.

The central portion of the façade of the Palacio del Rey Don Pedro presents a magnificent variety of craftsmen's decorative styles from different regions. (The overall design was later to be the inspiration for the gilt façade of the Cuarto de Comares in the Alhambra in Granada.) The lower level is constructed of rusticated masonry; the play of light on the surfaces accentuates the rough texture of the stone. On either side, the blind multifoil arches with *sebqa* tracery and decorative frames (the work of Sevillian master craftsmen) echo the decorations of the Giralda, the tower of Seville Cathedral nearby. The lintel above the main entrance was fashioned by craftsmen from Toledo; the voussoirs are embellished with rich *ataurique* and separated by thin strips of green tile. The central portion between the door and the windows is divided into three rectangular compartments by vertical bands with interlacing lines in green, black and white tile. Framed within this area is a recurring pattern of small multifoil arches with *sebqa* decoration. The space within the arches is filled with plant decoration alternating with a Kufic inscription, which reads: '*The empire for Allah*'. The *sebqa*-covered portions include emblems of Pedro the Cruel: lions, castles and coats-of-arms of the Order of the Sash. These same motifs appear in the central rectangle, although in lower relief and more finely drawn.

The next level is composed of a row of arched mullioned windows. The arches rest on coloured marble columns and the spandrels enclosed within their ornamental frames are embellished with interlaced motifs in polychrome tiles, also seen in the vertical divisions. This section of the façade is topped by a continuous frieze with inscriptions in Gothic and Kufic script. The Kufic inscription, which runs along the middle of the frieze, is repeated eight times, four from left to right in blue, and another four from right to left, backwards, upside down and in white. It reads '*And none is victor save Allah*', the motto of the Nasrid sultans of Granada. This inscription is surrounded by a legend giving the date of the construction of the palace: '*The highest, noblest and most powerful conqueror, Don Pedro, by God's grace King of Castile and León, has caused these Alcázares and palaces and these façades to be built, which was done in the year 1402*'. The date 1402 refers to the Spanish, or Caesarean, calendar, which begins in the thirty-eighth year after the birth of Christ; the façade can therefore be dated to 1364 of the Christian era.

The façade is framed by two masonry pillars, supported on columns and topped by two massive corbels which support the wooden cornice. The cornice was carved by craftsmen from Toledo and bears several friezes adorned with vegetal motifs, surmounted by small arch-like *muqarnas*. Kufic script between the columns reads: 'In grandeur and ostentation this house has no rival and Felicity attained.'

The doorway leads into the **entrance hall**, a rectangular room divided into three bays by arches supported on columns, three of which have Visigothic capitals; according to tradition, these capitals came from the former church of San Vicente, remains of which have been found in what is now the Patio de Banderas. The spandrels of these arches and the friezes decorating the walls are embellished with panels of stucco with plant and geometrical designs and *muqarnas* that once bore the emblems of Castile and legends in Kufic script – '*Felicity and prosperity [are] benefits of the sustainer [of all creatures] [Allah]; help [comes] from Allah; the greatness of Allah*' – and the words '*felicity*' and '*blessing*'. Of the wood-panelled ceilings in the entrance hall, only those in the end bays may be original, as the ceiling in the central bay, like the tile dados, dates from the restoration carried out in 1905. This area of the entrance hall was altered in the early nineteenth century, when a door was made to give direct access to the Dormitorio de los Reyes Moros from the Patio de las Doncellas. The door was bricked up during the restoration work of 1856 to 1857, when the plasterwork was painted in bright colours.

Following Islamic custom, the main parts of the Palacio del Rey Don Pedro are reached from the entrance hall via passages with right-angle bends. A small door at the right-hand side of the entrance hall leads to the private apartments. To the left is the entrance to the public areas. These are reached by crossing a square room with a late fifteenth-century panelled ceiling, passing through a door with a carved wooden lintel and fourteenth-century stucco, and following a narrow passage with a barrel-vaulted ceiling and walls bearing the inscription '*Glory to our lord the Sultan, Don Pedro! All praise to him!*'. A staircase off the passage leads to the upper floor and was once part of an Almohad building, as can be seen from its narrow arches supported on corbels. The fourteenth-century door at the end of the passage is decorated with inscriptions in praise of Allah.

The passage leads out into the **Patio de las Doncellas** (Courtyard of the Maidens), the centre of the official life of the court. It is rectangular and encompassed by a lower gallery of multifoil arches covered with *sebqa* decoration.

Below: Almohad tiles from the stairway of the Palacio del Rey Don Pedro

Opposite: vestibule ceiling

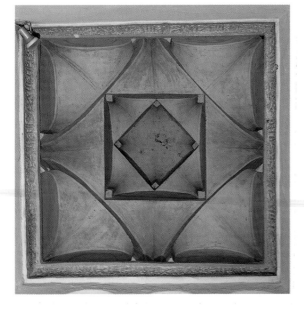 

Patio de las Doncellas,
general view (above)
and lower gallery (left)

Patio de las Doncellas, mosaic
dado (left) and detail (opposite)

These are in the Almohad tradition and originally had marble columns crowned
with wooden supports.

An original fourteenth-century feature is the decoration on the interior walls —
traditional Granada-style stucco on which reappears the Nasrid motto *And none is
victor save Allah* — and the mosaic dados with their interlaced designs (note especially
the magnificent patterning on the divan seats in the eastern wall). The ceilings, with
their geometrical pattern of eight-pointed stars, date from the reign of Isabella I
and were restored in 1856.

During the sixteenth century, the need to adapt the Palacio del Rey Don Pedro
to the requirements of the imperial court by making it more functional and more
comfortable, and by adding Renaissance embellishment, led to the launch of an
ambitious programme of works. Much of this was of a superficial nature,
consisting of the maintenance of structural and decorative elements or repairs to
superficial damage. However, the programme also included an enormously
ambitious project for the radical alteration of the appearance of the Real Alcazár.
Plans for this began to take shape in 1537, when Charles V established guidelines for
the royal building programme and appointed Alonso de Covarrubias and Luis de
Vega as architects with overall responsibility for the works. However, an effective
policy for construction work in the royal palaces was not implemented until 1545,
when the future Philip II of Spain set up the Council of Works and Forests and was
thus able to ensure that in every royal palace in Spain proper procedures for the
official supervision of works were established.

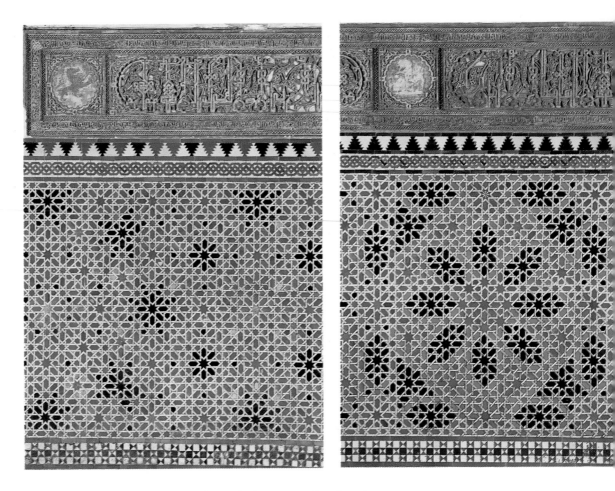

Patio de las Doncellas,
mosaic dado

However, plans for alterations to the Real Alcazár were already under way some
time before these regulations and supervisory arrangements came into effect. In 1532
Giangiacomo della Porta, Nicolao de Corte, Antonio María Aprile de Carona and
Antonio di Novo de Lancia, sculptors living in Genoa, were engaged to fashion a
series of columns, pillars, capitals, bases and lintels destined to transform the Patio
de las Doncellas. For reasons unknown this work was never carried out, although
the idea was revived two years later and a new contract signed with the sculptors
Aprile de Carona and Bernadino de Bissone, who were in Seville at the time, to
make a number of marble pieces for the gallery of the Patio de las Doncellas.
The materials for the upper gallery had to be sent from Genoa and did not reach
Seville until 1540, when work on the courtyard immediately began. Progress was
slow and the work was not finished until 1572, although it included renovations to
the upper series of rooms arranged around the courtyard. The aim was to provide
the king with apartments of the utmost artistic merit and physical comfort, and
some rooms were even equipped with fireplaces. The architect Luis de Vega was
responsible for planning the works while the master builder Juan Hernández, with
a large team of artisans and craftsmen at his command, was put in charge of
construction. For the upper gallery, Ionic columns where chosen, arranged so as to
emphasize the central openings on each side. The areas above the arches and within
the friezes were decorated with plasterwork with classical motifs, including the
Pillars of Hercules bearing the motto *Plus ultra* (Further), and various imperial
emblems. On the lower floor the great wooden doors and the ceilings to the rooms

adjacent to the Patio de las Muñecas were renewed and refurbished, and the corridors were paved with marble slabs.

These improvements were completed during the reign of Philip II; modernization facilitated access to its different areas so as to make of the royal palace a unified and rational whole. Following the preparation of a report on the state of the palace and the work required on it, from 1560 onwards a programme of alterations and repairs was put in hand to give a completely new look to the Patio de las Doncellas. First the original supports in the lower gallery were replaced by new ones, which were ordered in 1561 from the marble merchants Francisco and Juan de Lugano, together with others ordered from Francisco de Carona two years later. While the original supports were being replaced with Corinthian columns, the central arches in each gallery were raised to emphasize the central axis, and their masonry supports and plasterwork decorations were renewed.

At the top of each side of the courtyard a broad frieze was added; this bears such inscriptions as '*Praise be to Allah for his goodness*', '*Glory to our Lord*' and '*For you, O God without equal!* [is] *omnipotence*'. All these inscriptions date from the reign of Peter the Cruel. In the midst of them are the coats-of-arms of Castile and León, the Emperor Charles V, the Order of the Sash and the Pillars of Hercules bearing the motto *Plus ultra*. These emblems and motifs were added to the original Mudéjar scheme during the sixteenth century.

On the jambs to the central arches are seen Renaissance themes, including Plateresque balusters, female figures, urns, garlands, cherub heads and supports of various kinds with inscriptions. On the arch in the southern side of the courtyard, the inscriptions read '*de 16 L10, in ie and nf osis*' (on the right-hand jamb) and '*ma, plvs,*

Patio de las Doncellas, upper gallery, stuccowork (detail)

vltra' and '*Tanto monta*' (on the left-hand jamb). The outer face of this arch bears the date 1567. The inner side of the last arch in the south-eastern corner of the gallery has a bracket bearing the inscriptions '*R.F.P.II, 1569 a., Francisco, Martínez*' and '*M*'. The dates in these inscriptions refer to the years 1567-69, during the reign of Philip II, when the Renaissance decorative work was being carried out, under the direction of the master builder Francisco Martínez. The outer face of the large arch on the northern side of the courtyard bears the inscriptions '*koma, F.S. nl pan tro*' and '*o esfnl*'.

Opening onto the Patio de las Doncellas are three large rooms known as the Dormitorio de los Reyes Moros, the Salón del Techo de Carlos V, and the Sala del Almirante. The **Dormitorio de los Reyes Moros** (The Bedchamber of the Moorish Kings), so called because it may have been used for this purpose, lies on the northern side of the courtyard. It is entered through an arch with three ornate windows with openwork screens surrounded by inscriptions with such laudatory phrases as '*Praise be to Allah for his goodness*', '*Eternal salvation*' and '*Praise to Allah; for Allah glory be; the empire for Allah; thanks be to Allah*'. The main entrance has double wooden doors with interlacing motifs framed by a border bearing the inscription '*Happiness and prosperity and fulfilment of hopes*'. On the inside of the door is the inscription '*O, noble new dwelling! the blessed splendour [of your construction] was increased with the everlasting light of the most perfect beauty! Chosen shelter [where] feasts are held! It [is] the protection and the gift of [everything] that is good! Fountainhead of goodness and sustainer of valour! For you ...*'.

The Dormitorio de los Reyes Moros is divided into two areas. One is a spacious hall with plasterwork friezes, a carved and panelled wooden ceiling dating from the early sixteenth century, and two arched mullioned windows opening into the

Below and opposite:
Patio de las Doncellas, lower gallery, stuccowork (detail), and signature of Francisco Martínez

courtyard gallery. The other, to the right, is a square sleeping area, or alcove, separated by an arch resting on columns with white marble capitals. The alcove would have been closed off with curtains. A small door at the other end of the room leads into the private area of the palace. In the wall facing the door leading in from the courtyard are three horseshoe arches resting on two columns with Moorish capitals, framed by a decorative rectangle, or *alfiz*. The whole area around these arches is faced with *ataurique* stucco. This entrance leads to a second sleeping alcove identical to the one described above.

On the southern side of the courtyard is the **Salón del Techo de Carlos V** (Charles V Ceiling Room). This was used as the chapel of the Mudéjar palace, as shown by the Eucharistic prayer inscribed around the door, the composition of which is attributed by some scholars to St Bonaventura and by others to St Ildefonso of Toledo: '+ *anima: criste: santificame: corpus: criste: saluame: ¿qu a? Tu: est: cristus: librame: acalat... s.* [sic] *criste: laume: pasos: criste: confortame: obenes:* [sic] *ihesus: aude me: iniprimitas:* [sic] *separare: te: apostol: madino defendeme.'* Beside this is another inscription in Arabic script: '*Oh my trust! Oh my hope! You are my hope, you are my protector! Seal my works with goodness!'*. When the new oratory was added to the upper floor of the palace, this room was no longer needed for religious purposes, and the ceiling that gives it its name was installed between the years 1541 and 1543. The carving of the ceiling is attributed to Sebastián de Segovia and is one of the finest examples of its type in Spanish decorative art. Following a pattern given in the influential treatise on architecture by the Italian theorist Sebastiano Serlio, it consists of octagonal and square caissons decorated with rosettes; the central octagonal caissons are carved with busts of gentlemen and ladies, an allusion to the Emperor Charles V and Isabel of

Portugal. At the top of the walls are Renaissance motifs and imperial coats-of-arms with the motto *Plus ultra*. An arch with stucco decoration divides the room into two areas. The smallest was initially used as the chancel of the chapel but subsequently became a sleeping alcove. It has the same coffered ceiling as the larger area, and is lit by two mullioned windows, with original fourteenth-century decoration, which look out onto the courtyard. A shutter on the left-hand window bears the inscription '*Thus they were left in November 1856 after being repaired by A.N. de P.'*, which alludes to the stucco grotesques that adorn the window. The decoration of this room is completed by a tile dado surmounted by a frieze bearing depictions of castles and lions, escutcheons of the Order of the Sash and the Kufic inscription '*Glory to our lord the Sultan Don Pedro! May Allah protect him!'*.

A small door at the right-hand end of the room leads to the **Estancias de los Infantes** (Infantes' Rooms), which consist of three interconnecting areas and which were completely transformed in the nineteenth century. The central area was for some time used as a dining room and the stone commemorates the birth of the Infanta Doña María Isabel de Orléans y Borbón, which took place in that room on 21 September 1848. The two smaller areas at either the end of the central space were originally sleeping quarters, in the Moorish tradition. Doorways from the Estancias de los Infantes lead to the Jardín de la Galera (Garden of the Galley) and the antechamber of the Salón de Embajadores. The end room leads into the Salón del Techo de Felipe II.

The **Salón de Embajadores** (Ambassadors' Hall, or Throne Room), is the principal component of a suite of rooms used for official receptions and affairs of state. Among the historic events that have taken place here was the marriage of Charles V and Isabel of Portugal on 11 March 1526; here also was held the wake for the Count of Florida Blanca, who died in the Real Alcázar on 30 December 1808. Built on a square plan and having a hemispherical domed roof, the room follows the architectural scheme of a *qubba* (Islamic mausoleum), and is one of the areas of the palace that remain from the time of Abbad al-Mutamid, when it was known as the al-Turayya (Pleiades) room. The walls thus date from the eleventh century; the triple horseshoe arcades are framed by an *alfiz* and supported by pink marble columns with Moorish capitals, following a style that was used for the first time in the Hall of Abdul Rahman III, at Madinat al-Zahra. The Salón de Embajadores was redecorated and realigned when it was incorporated into the Mudéjar palace. It was then that the doorway to the Patio de las Doncellas was made and the pivoting doors were hung. These are decorated with interlaced patterns forming twelve-pointed stars; set into the main doors are smaller, horseshoe-arched doors. Each of the double doors is bordered by an inscription in Arabic on the outside and in Spanish on the inside. The Spanish inscription, in Gothic characters, gives the first verses of St John's Gospel and, with some modifications, extracts from Psalm 53. The Arabic inscription refers to the making of the doors in 1366 by craftsmen from Toledo. It reads: '*Our exalted high lord the Sultan, don Pedro, King of Castile and León (may*

Allah give him eternal happiness, and may it remain with his architect) ordered that these carved wooden doors be made for this room of happiness (which order was made for the honour and grandeur of his ennobled and fortunate ambassadors), from which springs forth an abundance of good fortune for this joyful city, in which palaces and Alcázares were raised; and these magnificent abodes [are] *for my lord and only master, who gave life to its splendour, the pious, generous sultan who ordered it to be built in the City of Seville with the help of his intercessor* [St Peter?] *with God the Father. In its dazzling construction and embellishment joy shone forth; in its adornment, craftsmen from Toledo* [were used]; *and this* [was] *in the exalted year 1404*

Salón de Embajadores, mosaic dado (left) and doors (opposite)

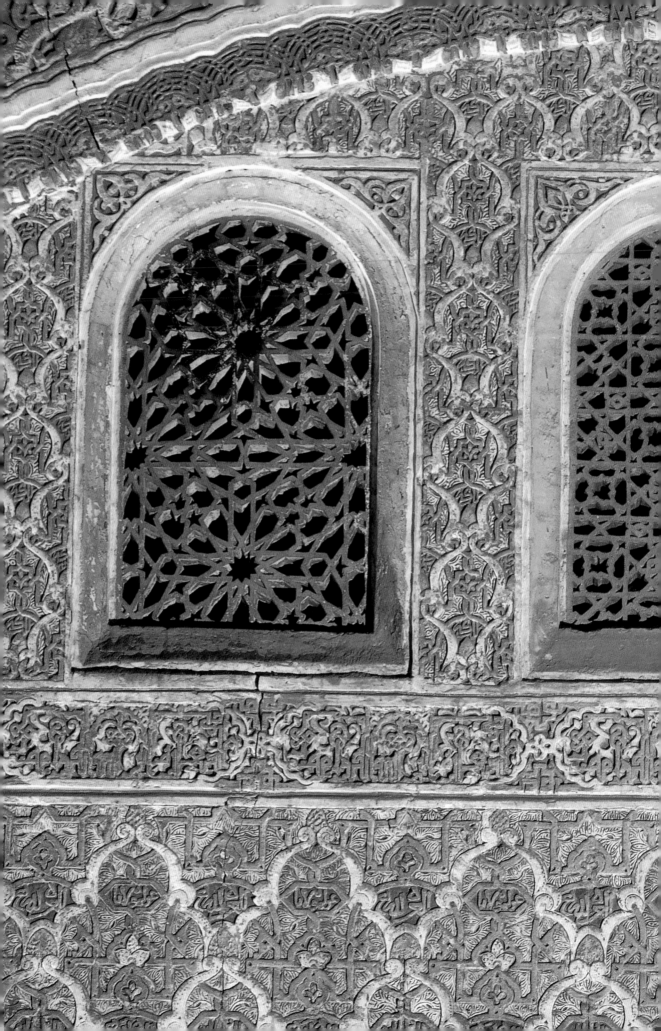

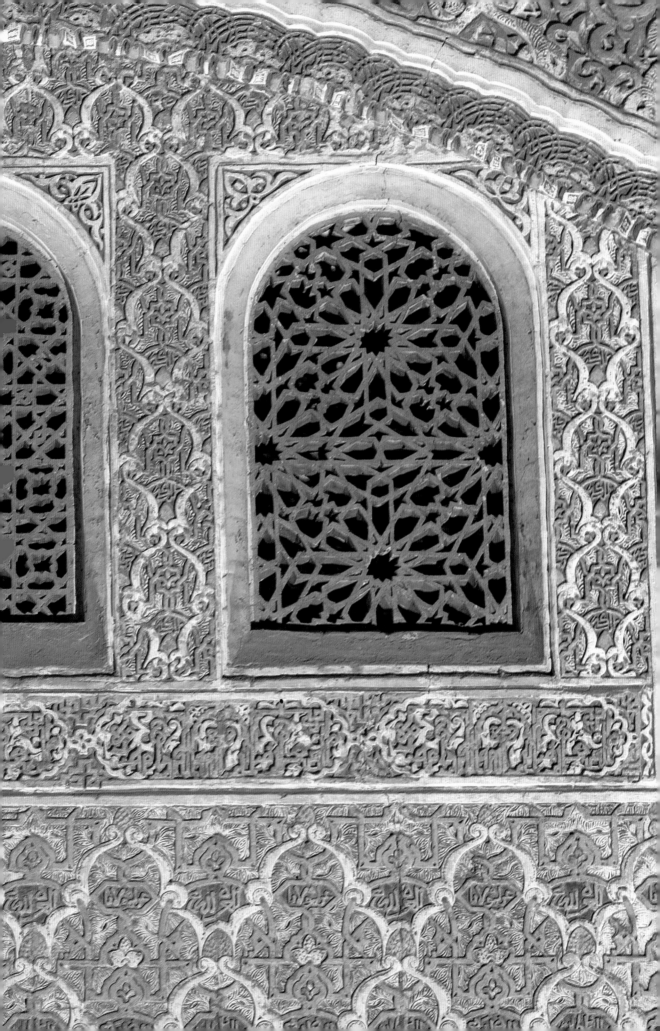

[AD 1366]. *Like the twilight at eventide and like the glow of dawn at morningtide* [is this work] *a throne resplendent with brilliant colours and the intensity of its magnificence ... praise be to Allah.*'

As the inscription states, the hall is resplendent with colour. On the dados tile mosaics from the Nasrid ornamental repertoire trace star-shaped and geometrical interlacing and undulating patterns in an array of contrasting colours. Above the dados are rich stucco panels with inscriptions to the glory of Allah and his protégé Peter the Cruel, which are repeated on the lower frieze. The corners of the room are decorated with carpet-like squares of plant motifs. These same motifs form a tracery inside the large multifoil arch that frames the horseshoe arches. Above the horseshoe arches are three latticework areas with geometrical patterns. All this is surmounted by two friezes, the lower of which is composed of forty-four small blind arches with a tracery of highly varied designs and motifs. The upper frieze consists of an interlocking pattern with truncated eight-point stars enclosing *ataurique* studded with escutcheons bearing the emblems of the house of Castile – the lion, the castle and the Orden de la Banda (Order of the Sash). This frieze is broken by four wrought-iron balconies that probably replace earlier arched windows. The balconies are supported by three elegant iron dragons made by the ornamental ironworker Francisco López between 1592 and 1597. Between the balcony doorways runs a gallery of small arches with Gothic tracery, framing portraits of the Castilian monarchs from Recceswinth to Philip III, painted by

Previous pages: Salón de Embajadores, stuccowork

Above: Diego de Esquivel, Galería de los Reyes Castellanos (1599), Salón de Embajadores

Opposite: Francisco López, balcony (1592-97), Salón de Embajadores

Diego de Esquivel in the late sixteenth century. At the very top of the wall, fine
Kufic inscriptions on a blue background, also by Diego de Esquivel, enclose
thirty-two female portraits, very likely princesses and infantas. Pendentives with
honeycombs of *muqarnas* support a magnificent wooden dome, at the centre of
which is a twelve-pointed star. During the restoration of 1843, when mirrors were
attached to the ceiling to add sparkle to the star, an inscription referring to the
construction of the dome was found; it was designed by Diego Ruiz in 1427 and
replaces an earlier one dating from the time of Peter the Cruel. It is without equal
in the history of Spanish architecture.

The **antechambers** adjoining the Salón de Embajadores lead into the Estancias
de los Infantes and the Patio de las Muñecas. These antechambers are notable not
only for their ceilings, made between 1590 and 1598 and attributed to Martín Infante,
but also the stucco friezes, which are the only examples of their type in the palace.
Among the *ataurique* decorations and Kufic inscriptions are medallions of various
shapes that enclose scenes from chivalry in white silhouette; men on horseback,
seated kings, warriors in combat or hunting, ladies and birds, combine with
fantastic animals and vine, oak or fig leaves, to evoke the fascinating world of
medieval pageantry. Certain authorities have distinguished two groups of artists
responsible for this figurative plasterwork; accordingly, the decorations in the left-

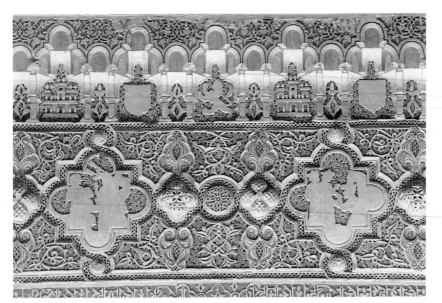

hand room, inspired by the *Crónica troyana*, a text dating from about 1350 that recounts the story of Troy illustrated with miniatures, may be attributable to masters from Toledo; these were then used by a group of Mudéjar artists from Seville to create the stucco decoration in the right-hand room, which shares subtle similarities with Islamic manuscript decoration and French ivories.

The **Salón del Techo de Felipe II** (Hall of the Philip II Ceiling), also known as the Salón de la Media Caña (Hall of the Curved Roof), is the final room that makes up the official area of the Mudéjar palace. It is located behind the Salón de Embajadores, and is the longest room in the entire Mudéjar palace. The wooden coffered ceiling, made during the reign of Philip II in the Mannerist style, is attributed to Martín Infante and is made up of square caissons enclosing alternating cruciform and square reliefs. The painting and gilding (since restored) was executed by Baltazar de Bracamonte. The most beautiful feature of the room is, however, the Arco de los Pavones (Arch of the Peacocks), the doorway into what was originally the Pleiades room of the Abbadid palace. The triple horseshoe arches resting on Moorish columns date from the 11th century. The ornamentation, dating from the reign of Don Pedro, consists of rich stucco; an array of Mudéjar motifs is combined with others of Islamic origin such as *ataurique*, Kufic inscriptions and interlaced patterns, together with such Christian additions as vine tendrils, scrolls and bird silhouettes. Yet other motifs, inspired by Persian textiles, have a more strongly Oriental flavour; among these are the peacocks in the spandrels that give the arch its name. These birds, like those arrayed along the lower frieze, have been linked to representations of birds in the palace at Tordecillas. The decoration of the room continues in the Mudéjar tile dados and what remains of the tiled original floor. Both were restored in 1896 by José Gómez de Otero with tiles from the workshops of the Jiménez brothers. During the 1980s parts of the floor were again restored with green and white glazed floor tiles.

The private areas of the Mudéjar palace are organized around the **Patio de las Muñecas** (Courtyard of the Dolls). By contrast to the Patio de las Doncellas, it is small and intimate in character. It is surrounded by a gallery that is asymmetrical in

design; the arches rest on Moorish columns of alternating white, black and pink marble. These materials were brought to Seville from Madinat al-Zahra by Abbad al-Mutamid. The plasterwork adorning the gallery, executed by craftsmen sent from Granada by Mohammed V, is a mixture of *ataurique* and *sebqa* ornamentation and is surmounted by a frieze consisting of small cusped arches. At the base of the arch nearest to the corridor, which leads to the entrance hall of the palace, are four small heads; these give the courtyard its name. One of the capitals of this arch, which is from the Moorish period, is inscribed with part of the second Sura of the Koran: '*in the name of Allah, your god* [is] *Allah, there is no god save Him, the Alive, the Eternal. Neither slumber nor sleep overtaketh him. Unto him belongeth whatsoever is in the heavens and whatsoever is in the earth. Who is he that intercedeth ...*'. The verse continues on another capital, possibly one of the capitals in the Salón de Embajadores on which the inscriptions are illegible. The continuation would have been: '*...with him save by his leave? He knoweth that which is in front of them and that which is behind them; while they encompass nothing of His knowledge save what He will. His throne includeth the heavens and the earth and He is never weary of preserving them. He is the Sublime, the Tremendous!*' Also originating from Granada are the tile mosaics on the dados and inscriptions, some with the Nasrid motto '*And none is victor save Allah*' and others dedicated to Peter the Cruel: '*O incomparable master, born of royal line!...May* [Allah] *protect him!...*'.

Between the sixteenth and seventeenth centuries an upper gallery was added to the courtyard, but this was removed in the mid-nineteenth century when the two upper floors were built and the courtyard was covered over with a glass roof. These alterations were directed by the architect Rafael Contreras, who was also responsible for restoration work on the Alhambra in Granada, where he made copies of the plaster-work and used them to decorate the walls of the courtyard.

Facing each other across the patio are two small rooms. The one on the western side, known as the **Sala de los Reyes Católicos** (Chamber of the Catholic Kings), leads into the Salón de Techo de Felipe II. It has a square floor plan and features Mudéjar plasterwork on the friezes and around the doorways. The arched, mullioned window (which looks out onto the Jardín del Príncipe, or Prince's Garden) and stucco were both made in the nineteenth century, and were copied from others elsewhere in the palace. Other interesting features of the room are the floor, made from bricks interspersed with original

decorative tiles, and the ceiling, with its marquetry of interlaced patterns. At the top of the walls are emblems of the Catholic Kings: the coats-of-arms of Castile and Aragón, with the eagle of St John, the yoke and the sheaf of arrows, and the motto *Tanto monta*. This decorative work evidently postdates the Reconquista of 1492, as the pomegranate which symbolized Nasrid Granada appears on the escutcheons and painted panels together with Renaissance candelabrum motifs.

The room on the eastern side of the courtyard is known as the **Sala de los Pasos Perdidos** (Room of the Lost Steps) and leads into the Dormitorio de los Reyes Moros. The stucco dates from the fourteenth century and the carved and inlaid ceiling dates from the fifteenth.

In the northern gallery of the courtyard is the entrance to the **Cuarto del Príncipe** (Prince's Suite), or **Dormitorio de la Reina** (Queen's Bedchamber). It was here, so history relates, that the ill-fated Prince John, the first son of Ferdinand and Isabella, was born in 1478. The room comprises a central area with a bedchamber, or alcove, at each end, and boasts interesting ceilings. The ceiling of the right-hand bedchamber is octagonal with a central eight-pointed star and triangular clusters of *muqarnas*. The tops of the walls are decorated with masks and candelabra and a lower frieze displays the coats-of-arms of Castile and Aragón, and the Orden de la Banda (Order of the Sash). The central, or main, room has a flat ceiling carved with geometrical interlaced patterns and bosses decorated with *muqarnas*. The ceiling of the left-hand bedchamber, a fine example of Sevillian craftsmanship, has square coffers decorated with pine-cone bosses and interlaced patterns separated by Renaissance mouldings. An inscription at the top of the wall records that '*this work was completed in 1543 by Juan de Simancas. Gilded and painted in the year 1854*'. The room is closed off by a wrought-iron gate facing onto the Jardín del Príncipe. Next to the gate is a stairway leading to the Oratorio de los Reyes Católicos on the upper floor.

The visitor returns towards the Patio de la Montería via the palace entrance hall, which is reached by a long narrow passage, divided in two sections with a right-angled bend. The passage is barrel-vaulted and decorated with *muqarnas*.

Patio del Crucero

The present-day appearance of the **Patio del Crucero** (Courtyard of the Crossing) is vastly different from the original scheme devised for it in Almohad times. It was originally built on two levels, with raised walkways intersecting in the centre and a walkway running round the four sides. On the lower level were covered galleries that served to support the walkways on the upper level. Within this covered area was a large central pool and beds in which grew aromatic plants and orange trees. This unusual arrangement often struck visitors to the Real Alcázar as curious and was particularly remarked upon by Andrea Navaggero, the Venetian Ambassador, who came to Seville to attend the wedding of Charles V. A more detailed and enthusiastic description of the courtyard was given at the beginning of the seventeenth century by the Sevillian cleric, antiquarian and poet Rodrigo Caro (1573-1646), who wrote that 'this patio, with its large areas open to the sky, its extraordinary elegance and its views of the subterranean garden, is both extremely pleasant and magnificent, while in summer the covered area below is the shadiest and coolest place one could imagine'.

Patio del Crucero, gateway

Patio del Crucero

The courtyard was badly damaged by the Lisbon Earthquake of 1755 and the sunken gardens had to be filled in to achieve a level with the upper walkways. As a result, the courtyard took on its present appearance; myrtle hedges enclose four areas in which palms, orange trees, rose bushes and other plants grow. This work was directed by the engineer Sebastián van der Borcht, who also built the gallery that links the Patio de la Montería with the Apeadero (Passenger Alighting Area), in which the main entrance to the Patio del Crucero is located. This gateway consists of a flat arch supported on pilasters, a broken pediment and an attic surmounted with a balcony, crowned by a curved pediment. The roof above the gateway is pierced by a dormer window. The same aesthetic principles of clear, sober lines combined with monumental solidity were applied to the southern side of the courtyard, where the medieval structure was strengthened by adding a gallery of paired columns with Ionic capitals and a groin-vaulted ceiling. A square arch, topped with the royal coat-of-arms and bordered with rock and cherub motifs, gives access to the Palacio Gótico.

The Palacio Gótico

The **Palacio Gótico** (Gothic Palace), also known as the **Salones de Carlos V** (Halls of Charles V), was built by Alfonso X in the second half of the thirteenth century and underwent a number of alterations during the sixteenth and eighteenth centuries. Originally it comprised four rooms: two long rooms of different widths, lying parallel to each other, and two smaller rooms placed across them at each end. All the rooms had ribbed vaulting, supported on embedded pillars, which were removed towards the end of the sixteenth century so that new tile facings could be put on the walls. The large central rooms were probably used for purposes of state. The small room to the right was used as a chapel, possibly that dedicated to St Clement in 1781; that to the left is now a library.

The exterior of the Palacio Gótico was of an extreme sobriety, evoking secular and religious Muslim buildings. It was set with crenellated buttresses and with corner turrets enclosing spiral staircases; because of these the palace was sometimes called the Cuartos del Caracol (Spiral Staircase Rooms). Some authorities have linked this type of arrangement to French Gothic building. It was within these walls that Alfonso X's erudite court circle created one of its most masterly poetic works: *Las Cantigas*. Profusely illustrated to aid comprehension, the book was worked on by a number of miniaturists, some of whom concentrated on the borders and architecture, whilst others painted in the animate figures. This division of labour explains the high output of richly illuminated manuscripts emanating from the palace's royal scriptorium. These include the *Crónica Real* (*Royal Chronicle*) and the *Book of Chess, Dice and Draughts*.

Salón de Tapices

During the reign of Philip II, the Palacio Gótico was extensively refurbished and the gardens behind the palace were made more accessible. The flat roofs were improved, the pillars supporting the vaulted ceilings were removed and high dados were applied to the walls. Asensio de Maeda, architect of Seville Cathedral, designed the corbels on which the ribs of the vaulting were supported and the ceramicist Cristóbal de Augusta created the splendid tilework dados. Not a trace of these alterations can be seen in the **Salón de Tapices** (Tapestry Room), which was completely rebuilt by Sebastián van der Borcht after the Lisbon Earthquake of 1755. It was he who installed the five bays of ribbed vaulting, with barrel arches supported on flat corbels, and a central lantern, which lights the interior. The decoration of the room was subsequently enriched by the addition of rectilinear and curvilinear plasterwork, and royal escutcheons in the Baroque manner.

The Salón de Tapices houses some of the twelve tapestries commissioned by Philip V, and woven by Francisco and Cornelio van der Gotten in the royal workshop during the mid-eighteenth century. These tapestries are copies of the *Conquest of Tunis* series, woven between 1548 and 1554 in the workshops of Willem Pannemaker; they follow designs by the Flemish painters Jan Vermeyen and Pieter

Coeck van Aelst. The tapestries comprise an extraordinary pictorial chronicle of this triumphant campaign, which was a central element in the myth created around Charles V and consolidated his reputation as a military hero. Unlike other pictorial records, in which allegory and symbolism might be employed, the aim in these tapestries was to be as objective as possible. As a result, banderoles and inscriptions play a vital role in the tapestries; they explain the pictorial content in a succinct form of narrative, the style of which has the detachment of a chronicle from that period. The desire for objectivity is such that inscriptions are even used to indicate the point from which the scene is being viewed. The series is also the first in which the rational concept of perspective, established during the Renaissance, was applied to the art of tapestry. Of all the tapestries in the series, the most striking is probably the first, *The Map of the Western Mediterranean, the North African Coasts and the Iberian Peninsula*, which provides a general view of the area in which the events took place. (Curiously, the map is reversed). A further indication of the quest for accuracy and objectivity is the figure of Jan Vermeyen on the right of the tapestry, who chose to show himself holding a geographer's compass. Other tapestries with such titles as *Reviewing the Troops in Barcelona*, *The Taking of Tunis* and *Going Aboard the Schooner* depict the main events of the campaign.

In the sixteenth century, the room parallel to the Salón de Tapices was known as the **Sala de las Bóvedas** (Vaulted Room) and also as the **Sala de las Fiestas** (Hall of

Opposite: Sala de las Bóvedas or
de las Fiestas

Below and overleaf: Cristóbal de
Augusta, tile dados (1577-78),
Palacio Gótico

Feasting). It was here that the festivities marking the marriage of Charles V and Isabel of Portugal took place. The room still retains its original ribbed vaulting but not the pilaster supports, which were replaced with corbels in 1577, when the tile dados were installed. These dados, an extraordinary display of polychrome glazed tilework, were designed by Cristóbal de Augusta in 1575. They are designed in the manner of a tapestry, with a lower frieze, a central panel framed by vertical borders, and two upper friezes. This compartmentalization is emphasized by monochrome border tiles and thin edging strips. The lowest ornamental band, with pairs of animals face to face, continues all round the room, as does the first of the upper friezes, which contains masks, snakes, birds and cherubs around an urn. The uppermost frieze displays the coats-of-arms of Spanish monarchs, with the Pillars of Hercules and the motto *Plus Ultra* supporting the virtues of Strength, Justice, Temperance and Prudence, as exemplified by Charles V.

The central panels of the dado are filled with a range of different motifs. There are flowers and animals, representations of the Spring of Life and scrolled medallions with busts of Charles V and Isabel of Portugal. Herms (classical busts set on pedestals, typical of the Mannerist style) separate the central panels; some of these represent Proteus, Mithras, Thought and Imagination, and are inscribed with the artist's name, AUGUSTA, and the dates 1577 and 1578. The yellow background contrasts with different shades of blue, and with the green, white and ochre in which the various motifs are depicted.

Above the dados the walls of the room are covered with banner-like hangings painted with heraldic motifs and themes relating to the Americas. These were

Cristóbal de Augusta, tile dados
(1577-78), Palacio Gótico

produced by Gustavo Bacarisas for the Ibero-American exhibition that was held in Seville in 1929.

The **Capilla del Palacio Gótico**, to the right of the Sala de las Bóvedas (Vaulted Room), has preserved its original ribbed vaulting. It, too, was renovated after 1577, when corbels designed by Asensio de Maeda and tile dados by Cristóbal de Augusta were installed.

The dados are set out in the same way as those in the Sala de las Bóvedas; they do not include heraldic or symbolic motifs but illustrate the theme of 'the Spring of Life' and feature a variety of grotesques. At the southern end of the Capilla is an unpainted wooden altarpiece with tapering pilasters made by Diego de Castillejo in the first half of the eighteenth century. Mounted on this is a painting of the Virgen de la Antigua, an anonymous seventeenth-century copy of the mural of this name in Seville Cathedral. The mirror-encrusted altar frontal and the plasterwork motifs on either side of the altarpiece date from the eighteenth century.

On the walls of the chapel hang a number of paintings with religious themes. These include *The Coronation of the Virgin*, by an anonymous Italian artist, *The Adulteress* and *Christ Robed as a Priest According to the Vision of the Blessed Mariana de Escobar*, all dating from the 17th century. *A Miràcle*, painted in about 1600, is traditionally attributed to Francisco Pacheco but is closer to the work of Alonso Vázquez. *The Virgin of the Kings between St Hermenengild and St Ferdinand* was painted by Domingo Martínez in 1742.

The small room to the left of the Capilla Gótica was originally known as the **Canterera** (Pitcher Room) and is now a library. It has nevertheless retained its ribbed vaulting and has tiled dados similar to those described above. Off the Pitcher Room, a room with a coffered ceiling made by Hernando de Zárate in 1576-77 leads into the gardens.

The Gardens

The gardens are one of the main attractions of the Real Alcázar. They developed from the Moorish vegetable gardens that were originally set out on the eastern side of the early Moorish palace.

The largest of the gardens is known as the Jardín de la Alcoba (Garden of the Alcoba) after the eleventh-century *qubba* that stood there. During Almohad times, this *alcoba* (from the Arabic *al-qubba*) was enclosed within the Alcázar's curtain wall, subsequently becoming the central point of the large open space within the outer fortress. This building would have had a square ground plan and a domed roof, as befitted its role as part of the royal cemetery of the Muslim sultans. After being remodelled in the mid-sixteenth century it came to be known as the Cenador de Carlos V (Pavilion of Charles V) and became a key element in the design of the gardens that were laid out over the area once covered by vegetable plots.

The gardens of the Real Alcázar are an outstanding example of the art of the Spanish garden. They combine Islamic traditions and Mannerist decorative traits with English landscape gardening, Romantic naturalism and a sense of history. The oldest gardens are those adjacent to the palace on the southern and western sides; the more recent gardens lie on the eastern side of the Almohad curtain wall and in the western part of the former Moorish vegetable garden.

Jardín del Estanque de Mercurio

The gardens lying within the original nucleus are clustered together without an overall plan. However, they do exemplify the deliberate fusion of the Hispano-Mooresque concern with compartmentalization with the quest for variety and spatial fragmentation that characterized Mannerism. They were created over a long period of time and magnificently express the dialectic between Art and Nature that was a central theme during the sixteenth and a large part of the seventeenth centuries. Rodrigo Caro, the seventeenth-century Spanish cleric, expressed this dialectic in his description of the New Garden, whose various plant species '*combine in a curious way with royal coats-of-arms, castles, lions, eagles and other figures with such grace and elegance that they appear to be paintings. And just as in painting the highest perfection is for the painting to imitate nature, here perfection consists in natural things appearing to have been painted.*' Other devices employed to give form to this paradox included figures from classical mythology, different types of water feature, simulated naval battles, contrived chaos, and imaginative topiary, all of which resulted in the unexpected and the playful. Caro describes this in some detail: '*there are such abundant water fountains and such slender pipes that when they are working it seems to be raining; all this is not only restful to the eye, but regales the ear with harmonious music from hidden organs artfully placed in all the grottoes... All the pathways through the gardens have a multitude of water spouts concealed in them to soak anyone who is too captivated with the beauty of the garden and the artful arrangement of the grottoes.*'

Jardín del Estanque

The large cistern, after which the **Jardín del Estanque** (Pool Garden) is named, was used to collect water to supply the Real Alcázar and for irrigation. Water was carried to the palace by a Moorish aqueduct known as the Caños de Carmona. The last section of the aqueduct made use of the encircling walls of the city, as can be observed in the Callejón del Agua, a narrow thoroughfare separating the Real Alcázar from the Santa Cruz neighbourhood.

On the northern side of the Jardín del Estanque is an arbour, or pavilion, and a building giving access to the Palacio Gótico; these were part of the work carried out on this part of the palace in 1575. The raised viewing gallery, consisting of round arches on marble columns with geometrical decoration in the spandrels, is the work of the Milanese architect Vermondo Resta. This arcade is dated 1612. The tiled panel depicting the royal coat-of-arms on the wall below the viewing gallery was designed by José Gestoso at the end of the nineteenth century.

The old cistern was converted into the present pool in about 1575. The pool was surrounded by an iron railing supported by marble pedestals topped by heraldic lions, and spheres supported by dolphins. Some of these are decorated with masks and are surmounted by pyramids. The metal adornments on the pedestals were once overlaid with gold; they were made by Diego de Pesquera and Bartolomé Morel, a metalworker, who also made the bronze fountain that stands in the centre of the pool. The figure of Mercury, the classical god of commerce, stands on an elaborate pedestal decorated with cherubs and monsters with spouts in their mouths.

Opposite: Diego de Pesquera y
Bartolomé Morel, Fuente de
Mercurio (1575)

Below: Vermundo Resta, Galería
del Grutesco (1612-21)

The figure forms part of an allegorical scheme, which portrays the wealth of Seville resulting from its status as a port and as the gateway to the New World. This theme is continued in the mythological paintings in the Galería del Grutesco. On the southern side, along the wall between the Pool Garden and the Jardín de las Damas, are seats faced with tiles. From this point a raised walkway runs parallel to the walls of the Real Alcázar in the direction of the Jardín del Príncipe. The walkway commands excellent views of the sixteenth- and seventeenth-century gardens.

On the western side of the Jardín del Estanque a flight of steps leads down to the Jardín de la Danza. It was laid in the eighteenth century and replaces a garden dating from the early seventeenth century.

Galería del Grutesco

The **Galería del Grutesco** (Grotto Gallery) is built into the ancient Almohad wall, which was renovated by Vermondo Resta between 1612 and 1621 in a rustic style. The section of it that provides a backdrop to the Jardín del Estanque and the Fuente de Mercurio (Fountain of Mercury) is in the manner of a triumphal arch; a lower level, with paired pilasters ending with corbels, supports an upper level arranged around tapering inverted columns, and provides a viewing gallery. All these architectural elements and wall areas are decorated with real and artificial rocks, which accentuate the Mannerist influences. The large niches on the lower level were once decorated with mythological and allegorical paintings executed by Diego de Esquivel in the late 1720s, whose subjects included Neptune and the Guadalquivir river. These paintings were retouched during the eighteenth century and were crudely repainted by Rosendo Fernández at the beginning of the twentieth century.

The gallery extends southwards along one side of the Jardín de las Damas and the Jardín de la Alcoba. This section of the gallery is arranged on two levels. The lower level, encrusted with rocks, has a series of panels decorated with paintings. The upper level consists of a gallery that incorporates marble columns of different periods and from different locations. Here stands a monumental fountain dedicated to Fame, with herms on its lower level.

The fountain was originally surmounted by an allegorical statue of Fame surrounded by other gods of classical mythology, and fitted with a water-driven mechanism that caused organ pipes to sound. In the lower gallery, there is a gateway that leads to the old vegetable garden of El Retiro.

Previous pages: Vermundo Resta, Galería del Grutesco (1612-21)

Above: Jardín de la Danza

Opposite: Fuente del Signo

Jardín de la Danza

The **Jardín de la Danza** (Garden of the Dance) is divided into two areas set on different levels. In the first area, starting at the stairs leading from the Jardín del Estanque, the focal point is formed by two marble columns on pedestals that once supported statues of Silenus and a dancing maenad. These figures, and the topiary nymphs and satyrs that once graced this space, give the garden its name.

The second area has a wide walkway with a small basin in the middle, decorated with tiles and supporting a sixteenth-century fountain. There are also four broad seats covered with modern, replica Renaissance tiles. Embedded in the walkways are small concealed water jets.

Entrance to the subterranean
gallery of the Patio del Crucero

Overleaf: The Baños de María
Padilla in the subterranean
gallery

At the northern end of the walkway is the entrance to the subterranean garden beneath the Patio del Crucero. The walls are faced with sixteenth-century polychrome tiles and the vault bears the vestiges of mural paintings of a similar date. At the southern end is the Jardín de las Damas. To the west are several large flowerbeds and a wall separating the Jardín de la Danza from the Jardín de Troya.

Jardín de Troya

An interesting feature of the **Jardín de Troya** (Garden of Troy) is its central fountain. The egg-and-dart pattern on the bowl and the lion-head water-spouts suggest that it is of Moorish origin and may date from the 10th century. The rustic-style gallery was constructed by Vermondo Resta in about 1606. It is the earliest example in the Real Alcázar gardens of the rustic style inspired by architectural treatises of the time and is clearly Mannerist in character. The Mannerist influence is also seen in the heads carved on the capitals above the pilasters of the gallery.

Jardín de la Galera

Opposite and below:
Jardín de Troya

The **Jardín de la Galera** (Garden of the Galley) is named after the galleys that, in the words of Rodrigo Caro, took part in '*imitations of naval engagements, bombarding each other with water cannons*'. Nothing of these galleys remains. Today the garden comprises four large beds planted with various flowers and shrubs. It is connected with the Estancias de Infantes, part of the Palacio del Rey Don Pedro, by a pergola

supported on pillars with Renaissance relief decoration. In the midst of the plants rises a marble column erected in homage of the poet-king Al-Mutamid; it is inscribed on one side with the words '*From the city of Seville to its poet-king Al-Mutamid Ibn Abbad on this ninth centenary of his sad banishment. 7 September 1091 – Rachab 384. Seville 1991.*', and on the other with the motto 'There is no god but God', and quotations from a poem in which the king expresses his longing to return to the gardens of his 'blessed palace': '*God grant that I may die in Seville and that our graves be opened there at the resurrection.*' But it was the inhospitable African soil at the foot of the Atlas Mountains that would witness his death and receive him into its bosom.

Jardín de las Flores (Jardín de la Gruta Vieja)

A wall pierced by a central arch separates the Jardín de la Galera from the **Jardín de las Flores** (Garden of Flowers), also known as the Jardín de la Gruta Vieja (Garden of the Old Grotto). Against the wall is a tank faced with richly-coloured Seville tiles, dating from the sixteenth and seventeenth centuries. The water-spout is set in a grotto surrounded by rustic motifs. Another grotto, after which the garden is named, was built on the western side of this space at the end of the sixteenth century; it was decorated with a variety of figures, shells and other marine motifs. This grotto was reconstructed in the early seventeenth century by Vermondo Resta, who redesigned it in a style inspired by Giacomo da Vignola, the influential

Italian Mannerist; two pairs of rusticated masonry pilasters flank a niche, crowned
by a gable and containing a bust of Charles V.

Jardín del Príncipe

This garden is named in memory of Prince John, the first child of Ferdinand and
Isabella, who was born in the adjacent Cuarto del Príncipe, part of Palacio del Rey
Don Pedro. In the mid-sixteenth century a considerable amount of building work
was carried out, which was then substantially altered by Lorenzo de Oviedo after the
Jardín del Príncipe was built in the late sixteenth century. This comprises a double
tier of eight arches, each supported by Doric columns on the lower level and Ionic
columns on the upper. Between them is a mezzanine with windows separated by
pilasters. The wooden ceilings were made between 1592 and 1595, possibly by the
master carpenter Martín Infante. The remaining two sides of the garden are the
result of alterations carried out in the 1970s.

Jardín de las Damas

The **Jardín de las Damas** (Ladies' Garden) was already in existence in the sixteenth
century, albeit on a smaller scale. At the beginning of the seventeenth century
Vermondo Resta extended and redesigned it; according to his scheme the garden
was laid out as a large rectangle with eight compartments along a central axis with

Vermondo Resta, windows (left) and gateway (below), Jardín de las Damas

Opposite: Fuente de Neptuna, Jardín de las Damas

fountains at the intersections of the paths, the whole bordered by a wall with gateways and windows inspired by Vignola. While the fountains at the ends of the paths are set close to the ground, the central fountain is of monumental proportions. It is crowned by a statue of Neptune in the style of Giovanni da Bologna. Four grottoes were built in the surrounding wall and adorned with earthenware mythological figures and shell, conch, and coloured glass decorations. Other figures were once cut out of the myrtle hedges, to which painted wooden hands and heads were added. These topiary figures included Hercules struggling with Antaeus, the Judgement of Paris, Proteus and Phorcos, and Diana and Actaeon, as well as the coats-of-arms of the Spanish royal house.

The eastern side of the garden is enclosed by the Galería del Grutesco. As in the Jardín de la Danza, the alleys in the Jardín de las Damas have water-spouts cleverly hidden among the paving stones: when turned on, the jets form a shimmering watery arcade.

Jardín del Laberinto Viejo

The **Jardín del Laberinto Viejo** (Old Maze Garden), also known as the Jardín de la Cruz (Garden of the Cross), is reached from the Jardín de las Damas by the Puerta de Hércules (Gateway of Hercules) and from the Jardín de las Flores by a small gate in the wall. Its name alludes to the intricate maze fashioned out of clipped hedges. In the middle of the maze was a pond surrounding an artificial mound; this arrangement symbolized Mount Parnassus. At the summit stood statues of Apollo, the Nymphs and Pegasus, with other figures on the slopes, some serving as water-spouts. A series of automata completed the accoutrements of this remarkable garden. The maze was removed in 1910 on the orders of Alfonso XIII and the garden is now completely different.

Jardín de Laberinto Viejo,
Puerta de Hercules (left)
and Mount Parnassus (right)

Jardín de la Alcoba

The summer house, or pavilion, that is the major feature of the **Jardín de la Alcoba**
(Garden of the Alcoba) was converted from the *qubba* that originally stood here.
The conversion was carried out between 1543 and 1546; the date is marked on the
paving stones together with the name of Juan Hernández, the master builder of the
Real Alcázar, who supervised the work. The result is a symbolic edifice extolling the
fame of the Emperor Charles V. The building is a fusion of Mudéjar and
Renaissance elements and is characterized by geometrical rigour, harmony,
refinement and a sense of proportion. It is the work of a small army of artisans and
craftsmen, including the bothers Diego and Juan Polido, who were responsible for
the very varied glazed tiles and ceramic components of the decorations to walls,
floors and parapets. It is not known who fashioned the splendid capitals to the outer
galleries, although it is thought that they are of Genoese origin and may be linked to
Antonio María Aprile de Carona and Bernardino de Bissone. The pillars appear to
be Moorish. Inside the summer house, the most remarkable feature is the floor, with
its geometrical and floral patterns; a plan created in black and white tiles shows the
layout of an earlier maze in the Real Alcázar gardens. A fountain in the centre of the
pavilion fills the building with the invigorating freshness and soothing sound of
gushing water. The overflow from the fountain is carried away from the building by
a small channel. The wooden coffered ceiling is supported on pendentives and bears

Transportation Security Administration

NOTICE OF BAGGAGE INSPECTION

To protect you and your fellow passengers, the Transportation Security Administration (TSA) is required by law* to inspect all checked baggage. As part of this process, some bags are opened and physically inspected. Your bag was among those selected for physical inspection.

During the inspection, your bag and its contents may have been searched for prohibited items. At the completion of the inspection, the contents were returned to your bag.

If the TSA security officer was unable to open your bag for inspection because it was locked, the officer may have been forced to break the locks on your bag. TSA sincerely regrets having to do this, however TSA is not liable for damage to your locks resulting from this necessary security precaution.

For packing tips and suggestions on how to secure your baggage during your next trip, please visit:

www.tsa.gov

We appreciate your understanding and cooperation. If you have questions, comments, or concerns, please feel free to contact the TSA Contact Center:

Phone: 866.289.9673 (toll free)
Email: TSA-ContactCenter@dhs.gov

* Section 110(b) of the Aviation and Transportation Security Act of 2001, 49 U.S.C. 44901(c)-(e)

Rev. 8-1-2004

Smart Security Saves Time

Transportation Security Administration

NOTIFICACIÓN PARA INSPECCIÓN DE EQUIPAJE

La Gestión de Seguridad de Transporte (TSA por sus siglas en inglés) está obligada bajo la ley de inspeccionar todo el equipaje registrado para protegerlo a usted y a sus compañeros pasajeros. Como parte del proceso, algunas maletas se abren e inspeccionan físicamente. Su maleta fue seleccionada entre otras para dicha inspección física.

Es posible que durante la inspección, su maleta y su contenido fueran inspeccionados para averiguar si incluían artículos prohibidos. El contenido de su maleta se colocó nuevamente en su maleta cuando se terminó la inspección.

Si el inspector de TSA no pudo abrir su maleta para fines de inspección porque estaba cerrada con llave, es posible que haya tenido que romper la cerradura de su maleta. La Gestión de Seguridad de Transporte (TSA) lamenta sinceramente haber tenido que hacerlo, sin embargo, TSA no es responsable por los daños a sus cerraduras que resulten de esta precaución de seguridad necesaria.

Por favor visite el sitio de la Web siguiente para obtener consejos prácticos y sugerencias de cómo asegurar su equipaje durante su próximo viaje:

www.tsa.gov

Le agrademos su conformidad y cooperación. Si tiene alguna pregunta, comentario o inquietud sobre este asunto, póngase en contacto con el Centro de Contacto de TSA llamando al:

Número de Teléfono: 866-289-9673 (gratuito)
Correo electrónico:
TSA-ContactCenter@dhs.gov

*Sección 110(b) de la Ley de Seguridad de Aviación y Transporte de 2001.
49 U.S.C. 44901(c) (0)

Rev. 8-1-2004

La seguridad inteligente ahorra tiempo

⋆ U.S. Government Printing Office 2006-324-160

the imperial coats-of-arms, and the darkness of the wood contrasts with the rich colours of the high dados and stucco friezes.

The Jardín de la Alcoba is bordered on its eastern side by the Galería del Grutesco. This is pierced by the Puerta de Privilegio (Privilege Gate), a fine doorway inspired by designs published by Vignola, which once opened onto the vegetable gardens of El Retiro but now leads through to the later gardens that replaced them.

On the western side of the Jardín de la Alcoba is the **Cenador del León** (Lion Pavilion), a small mid-seventeenth-century structure attributed to Diego Martín de Orejuela. It was originally decorated with mural paintings, which enhanced the brilliance of the tiles covering the domed ceiling. In front of the pavilion is a fountain with a lion. The circular basin is decorated with large water-spout masks from which water flows into a large rectangular pool. Both the fountain and the lion, from whose jaws water gushes, predate the pavilion itself.

The garden is luxuriant with vegetation; the trees and large shrubs are all recent additions, as are such exotic plants as China-berry, Judas trees, Chorisia or palo borracho, magnolias, palm trees, bamboo and jojoba. Original and evocative combinations were produced by planting these species side by side with more traditional types such as orange trees, jasmine, laurels, rosemary, lavender, philadelphus and rose bushes. Originally, however, according to the custom of the

Pabellón de Carlos V (opposite),
with its floor showing the
signature of Juan Hernández
(right) and tiles by Diego and
Juan Pulido (below)

Above: Diego Martín de Orejuela, Cenador del León

Opposite: Pabéllon de Carlos V, ceiling (above) and floor with plan of the maze (below)

sixteenth and seventeenth centuries, only low-growing species were cultivated to ensure that the architectural features of the gardens could be appreciated to the full. The topiary figures could then easily be seen in all their geometrical precision from the top of the Galería del Grutesco and the Jardín del Estanque. Today, it is the colourful flowers, the scents of aromatic plants and the shade-giving trees that make these gardens so enchanting.

New Gardens

The new gardens were laid out and developed in the nineteenth century on the site of the old Alcoba and El Retiro vegetable gardens. At the behest of Queen Victoria Eugenia, an English-style garden was created on the western side of the Jardín de la Alcoba. With its Romantic inspiration, the Jardín Inglés is in complete contrast to the others in the Real Alcázar: whereas these are characterized by compartmentalization, secluded areas, geometric rigour and tightly controlled vegetation, the Jardín de Estilo Inglés is a space with broad perspectives where plants grow freely, as conceived by a landscape gardener. Unpaved paths wind in and out of bushes, which contrast with grassy expanses where trees are planted apparently at random; these are very varied and include cedar, yew, oak, horse chestnut and some very rare species, such as the ginkgo bilova from eastern Asia.

In front of the Alcoba pavilion and surrounded by the English garden on two sides is the **Laberinto** (Maze), designed in 1914 in the Renaissance style. Its clipped hedges replace earlier ones which had been uprooted four years before. Behind it, in a corner formed by the new Real Alcázar wall separating the English garden from the Paseo de Catalina de Ribera and the Calle San Fernando, is a tower that was originally a part of the defensive fortifications of the city in Almohad times.

The old vegetable garden of El Retiro was converted into a park in two separate stages. The first stage, from 1913 to 1917, during the reign of Alfonso XIII, resulted in the creation of the present **Jardín del Retiro** (El Retiro Garden). In the second stage, from 1956 to 1958, the **Jardín de los Poetas** (Poets' Garden) was made to designs by Joaquín Romero Murube, the Sevillian poet and curator of the Alcázar; he followed the aesthetic principles of the romantic garden and the ideas applied by Jean Forestier in his work on the Parqué de Maria Louisa (Park of Maria Louisa) and the estate of the Marquess of Castilleja de Guzmán. He designed some sections of the park with hedge-lined pathways and an irregular plan, which he combined with an area, symmetrically laid out, parallel to the Jardín del Retiro. For the Jardín de los Poetas he designed two large pools, also surrounded by hedges, and placed a fountain from the convent of Sanlúcar de Barrameda between them. A column at each end of the central path emphasizes the sense of symmetry and perspective, which is further accentuated by lines of cypress trees and low hedges; these are interspersed with stone and iron seats between pedestals supporting urns, which impose lateral limits to the scheme.

The **Jardín del Retiro** was laid out while the Marquess de la Vega Inclán was curator of the Real Alcázar. It was designed by José Gómez Millán, who took the regular layout of the Jardín de las Damas as a model. A grid of squares, cut away at the corners, was laid out with walkways between them; in some sections these have water courses running along them, linking the fountains at the intersections.

Above: Jardín de los Poetas

Below and opposite: Puerta Privilegio, Jardín de los Poetas

Jardín del Retiro (opposite)
and the pergola (above)

Urns on pedestals and tile-clad benches and balustrades completed the design,
which has broad perspectives, thanks to the judicious placing of trees and shrubs.
A pergola was also built above one of the water-wheels that once irrigated the
Moorish vegetable gardens.

Puerta de Marchena

The **Puerta de Marchena** (Marchena Gatehouse) takes its name from the gate to
the palace of the Dukes of Arcos in the village of Marchena, near Seville, that was
bought at auction by Alfonso XIII, brought to the Real Alcázar in 1913 and erected
there by the architect Vicente Traver.

The gatehouse, in which heraldic motifs are a prominent element, is a superb
example of late fifteenth-century Gothic art. The doorway is flanked by columns
ending in pinnacles, which are in turn framed by columns with spiral fluting.
Tracery adorns the space between the doorway and the inner pillars and clove motifs
fill the area between the inner and the outer columns.

Of particular interest are the statues of savages supported by brackets on either
side of the door, made by the French-born sculptor Esteban Jamete in 1544. They
hold maces and shields with coats-of-arms: those of the Ponce de León family on
the left, and those of the Figueroa y Fernández de Córdoba family on the right.
Other heraldic elements include the lion above the door, an eagle and lion crowning

the pinnacles and two escutcheons on each side of the area of wall below the window. One escutcheon has the armorial bearings of Ponce de León and the other has those of Pacheco. This suggests that the gatehouse was built during the years before Don Rodrigo Ponce de León, first Duke of Arcos, came to the throne, when his grandmother Beatriz Pacheco acted as his guardian.

Pabellón de la China and the Patio de la Alcubilla

The **Pabellón de la China** (China Pavilion) was built in the early nineteenth century. It takes its name from the dinner service and Oriental porcelain used at royal banquets held at the Real Alcázar.

The **Patio de la Alcubilla** (Courtyard of the Cistern) is also known as the Patio del Tenis (Tennis Courtyard) because a tennis court was made there for Alfonso XIII and Queen Victoria Eugenia in the early twentieth century. Its present appearance is the result of radical alterations carried out in the 1970s. Four flower-beds are separated by pathways; at the centre is an early seventeenth-century marble fountain. This was brought to the Royal Palace from the former residence of the Sánchez Dalp family, based in the Plaza del Duque de la Victoria in Seville.

The buildings on the northern side of the courtyard form part of the **Cuarto del Sol** (Sun Suite). Part of a Mudéjar arcade remains at the entrance to the suite from the Apeadero (Alighting Area).

Cuarto del Sol gallery

Apeadero

The **Apeadero** (Alighting Area), where carriages stopped to take up and set down passengers, was designed by the Milanese architect Vermondo Resta in 1607 and was completed two years later. A gateway to the Patio de Banderas was constructed, which would give access to the palace from that side. The Apeadero consists of aisles: a broad central aisle and two narrower ones with arches supported by paired Tuscan columns. The side walls, which follow a similar scheme, have pilasters surmounted by arches embedded in the wall and spandrels filled with geometrical reliefs. The flat ceiling is supported by wooden beams. The basilica-like design of this majestic hall bears a close resemblance to some of Resta's ecclesiastical buildings.

On the wall at the head of the central aisle is an altarpiece of gilt and painted wood, with a late seventeenth-century scene of the Presentation of the Virgin in the

Vermondo Resta,
Apeadero (1607-9)

Temple flanked by spirally fluted columns. A staircase in the west wall of the Apeadero leads up to the first floor, and a room that was used as an armoury during the reign of Philip V.

The main entrance to the Apeadero is also the work of Vermondo Resta, but was altered in the eighteenth century, as recorded on a marble tablet above the door. The inscription reads: '*When Philip III was King of Spain this building was erected in the year MDCVII. It was repaired, extended and used as a Royal Armoury in the reign of Philip V in the year MDCCXXIX.*' In this refined façade, Resta displays his understanding of the language of classicism and his ability to bend the rules when the occasion required. The upper opening looks somewhat unsophisticated, but was probably affected by the alterations carried out in the 18th century. On the gable end is a wrought iron crown above a tiled panel, which displays the coat-of-arms of Philip V. This panel, made by a local pottery after a design of 1889 by José Gestoso, replaces an earlier painting that had fallen into disrepair.

The gate opens onto the Patio de Banderas, a large area where street fairs were once held to celebrate royal visits and commemorative events related to the royal family. From this square, filled with the scent of orange blossom and the sound of a murmuring fountain, the visitor can enjoy a fine view of Seville's great Gothic cathedral and its elegant tower, the Giralda.

Previous pages: Patio de Banderas

Opposite: Vermondo Resta, Apeadero, main entrance (1607-09)

Index